DESTINATION JOY

ARE YOU LIVING A LISTLESS, JOYLESS LIFE?
FRIEND, GOD HAS MORE FOR YOU!

PEGGY R. NICHOLSON

We enjoy hearing from our readers. Please contact us at www.anekopress.com/questions-comments with any questions, comments, or suggestions.

Illustrator: Lorena Orvananos
Editor: Charlene Miskimen

Aneko Press
www.anekopress.com
Aneko Press, Life Sentence Publishing, and our logos are trademarks of Life Sentence Publishing, Inc.
203 E. Birch Street
P.O. Box 652
Abbotsford, WI 54405
RELIGION / Christian Living / Spiritual Growth
Paperback ISBN: 979-8-88936-274-6
eBook ISBN: 979-8-88936-275-3
10 9 8 7 6 5 4 3 2 1
Available where books are sold

In *Destination Joy*, Peggy Nicholson reveals the sometimes-hidden secret to a life of constant joy and peace. Beginning with her conversion experience with Christ, she traces her personal discovery of the eternal principles that fill our lives with abundance. This book is a must-read for anyone seeking a deeper, more meaningful relationship with Jesus.

Dr. Russ Barksdale Ph.D,
Pastor Emeritus Rush Creek Church

The tools and resources of God are actual. They are real. His Word, prayer, worship, fellowship, and witness all play a vital role in our abiding in Him. And when we do, we experience peace and joy like never before. How sad that so many Christians never discover this wonderful truth!

Peggy Nicholson, in *Destination Joy*, does such a winsome job of leading us to experience the rich fullness of God in our lives on a daily basis. My prayer is that you will step out in faith and begin to practice these helpful reminders from God's Word. When you do, you'll start on the greatest adventure we can have this side of Heaven!

Dr. John B. Sorensen
President/CEO, Evangelism Explosion International

My wife and I have known Peggy and Art for almost thirty years. She is a practitioner of what she teaches. When I introduced Evangelism Explosion to our church, Peggy was my first trainee. When our church launched initiatives to serve the poorer areas of our city with the highest crime rates, Peggy volunteered to mentor young women. She is a teacher, mentor, evangelist, and servant. I highly recommend this book!

Dr. David Self
Board Chair, Evangelism Explosion International

Peggy Nicholson has devised a path that you can follow to achieve these goals in *Destination Joy*! Through transparency and honesty, she shares the struggles she has overcome to reach those desires personally. I wholeheartedly recommend this book to anyone who is seeking to grow in their relationship with the Lord.

Mary Ann Bridgwater
Pray the Word Ministries

CONTENTS

To Polly Dawson, my friend and mentor: Thank you for tirelessly leading others to the bountiful "Well of Living Water."

CHAPTER 1

SO NOW WHAT?

No discipline seems pleasant at the time, but painful. Later on, however, it produces a harvest of righteousness and peace for those who have been trained by it.
Hebrews 12:11

When I invited Jesus Christ into my heart in college, I was thrilled. That experience transformed me. But then, as I left the safety net of my new church and friends, I began to fumble. Now what? How do I grow up? Sadly, I didn't find that answer for quite a few years. I stumbled around aimlessly in the wilderness. I began to miss church. I picked up my Bible only when all else failed. I prayed "this is what I need and want" prayers. I lived a flat, listless Christian life.

If you too are living a bland, colorless spiritual life, you will be frustrated and disappointed in your Christian journey. Beloved, this is not God's plan for you and me. If you are gloriously saved and forgiven from a lifetime of sin, that's a great beginning; but trying hard to live the abundant life is impossible in the flesh. That's why our gracious God left us the Counselor, the Holy Spirit, who breathes life into our dry bones. He is leading us to live exceedingly and abundantly beyond what we could have imagined for ourselves, and He calls us daily into obedience. And He often calls us to move in places we feel squeezed. This is where I find myself. It is not my desire, my passion, or my gifting to write, but I feel I would sin if I did not at least try to convey the life-changing disciplines God has taught me, the answers to my "so now what?" questions.

But don't you just hate discipline? I mean, really! I'd rather just eat bonbons and lounge on the couch. If there were a way to make money, lose weight, clean the house, or do anything else important from the couch, I'd do it! Unfortunately, not a lot of satisfaction and purpose comes from the couch. Well, maybe a little! But most of the things that have mattered to me, oddly enough, came from good old-fashioned hard work. Think about it! What in your life that matters deeply to you came from the couch?

Honestly, there's only one reason why I write this book: I am compelled by the Holy Spirit to get off the couch. Compelled to write down what God has taught me over the last few decades. Compelled not to squander His lessons, His "on the job" training. Compelled to share with you how to get off your own couch!

I have witnessed God change lives before my eyes. I've

seen marriages resurrected from the dead. I have seen broken people *unbreak* because of the overwhelming power of God's Word and principles. He created us for one reason: to have a love relationship with Him! That's it! If we miss this principle during our time here on earth, we've missed it all. God desires an abiding relationship with us. He is calling us into intimacy. He's calling us to discipline. He's calling us to get off our couches.

You may be asking, "How does building intimacy with God affect me? How does an abiding love relationship with my Creator God benefit me?" It's a fair question. So let me ask you, what do you really want? What is your deepest desire? I think it's safe to say we all want peace in the midst of turmoil. We'd love a rock-solid foundation under our feet when the storms come. We all desire joy in the midst of sorrow. We want comfort and rest in our losses. We all want to be loved unconditionally. We want to be known, really known. I think we can agree that everyone would like to hand over the stressful reins of their lives to a loving and perfect God, to rest in His arms, trusting that He is in control of all and that He loves us completely in spite of our faults and imperfections. If this is your heart, then let's talk about how to get there. It will take intentionality. We'll have to get off our couch and begin!

You are not your own; you were bought at a price (1 Corinthians 6:19-20). So, what does that mean? I am not my own? Many of us assume that our time is our own. We plan our day. We decide how we will spend our time. After all, it's our time, isn't it? We have responsibilities. We need to get up, get ready for work, go to work, interact with our families, eat meals, get some sleep. If we are Christians, we will also include Bible studies, church, and maybe some ministry work. Clearly, we are able to fill our time.

If we are not careful, the troubles of the world will easily crowd out our good intentions to build intimacy with our Creator. If we are thinking that spending quality and quantity time with God is just another box to check, we will give up before we even begin. Is your personal time with Christ your main priority? Sitting at the feet of Christ, listening and speaking to Him, is not a box to check. It is our lifeblood. It is not an option. We don't decide, "I think I'll spend time with God today. I think I can work Him into my busy schedule." Our only decision as believers is, "I must spend time at the feet of the cross. I must get to know my Lord and Savior. I must listen and sit at His feet."

So why should you spend your time reading this book? If you are hungering for a deeper intimacy with your Savior, there are clear principles.

Before I married, as a young believer, I often prayed arrow, or impromptu, prayers throughout the day, believing I was praying without ceasing. I spent time in church, in Bible studies, and in prayer groups. I had a genuine passion for the Lord, but as I was to find out, I was just skimming the surface. Fortunately for me, my husband had been walking solidly with the Lord for many years. He quickly recognized some gaps in my spiritual walk. He challenged me to think of my relationship with the Lord as like our marriage. He explained, "If I told a friend that

I loved my wife but couldn't answer simple questions about you, he might conclude I don't really love you. For example, I don't know where you work, what kind of car you drive, where you grew up, or your parents' names." This simple illustration helped me reevaluate my relationship. Even though I was saved and committed to the Lord, I was not growing significantly. I was giving God my leftovers. I was waving at Him as I ran out the door. I was blowing kisses at Him and telling Him how I loved Him as I blew past Him onto my daily activities.

A lot of these activities were, in fact, necessary. I had to go to work, had to take care of family members. I had friendships and social times to consider. But building a relationship with God was taking a backseat. I was trying to make a successful marriage out of being around Him, but not consistently and intentionally being with just Him. I perceived that my church, Bible study, and erratic prayer times were enough.

Intimacy is developed as we seek to know one another. Jeremiah 29:13-14 says, *You will seek me and find me when you seek me with all your heart. I will be found by you.* God desires this kind of relationship as He urges us to seek Him daily. As we all know, building intimacy with someone takes intentional quality and quantity time. I cannot merely wave at my husband and expect to know and be known. John 17:3 says, *Now this is eternal life: that they know you, the only true God, and Jesus Christ whom you have sent.* So here's the challenge. Do you really want to know Him? It will take intentionality on your part. It will take time. In the front of my Bible, I have written the words, "I have decided to follow

Jesus, no turning back!" Deciding! That's half of the battle. Have you decided?

My husband and I have enjoyed facilitating a marriage class for quite some time. We have had a front-row seat to some awe-inspiring transformations. Four years ago, Lisa came to me after attending our marriage class. We met for lunch where she wept through our entire meeting, claiming she was leaving her husband and saw no hope. She felt guilty because she had a young child at home. Now, I am not a trained counselor, but the principles that God teaches in His Word are clear. After a few meetings with her, she began to follow the simple plan I have outlined in this book. It is not new, but it is foolproof. Allowing God to transform *you* from the inside will revolutionize your life in every way. If we become the best version of ourselves that we can, then those around us will likely change too. But either way, we will be renewed, revived, and changed by an intimate daily encounter. He will heal our broken places if we give Him a chance. Spending time with God is the key to spiritual and mental health.

Over the years, I have also developed a mentoring ministry that has allowed me to participate with God in some crazy, life-changing dramas. It's been an honor and a privilege to watch God transform lives.

I particularly remember a young, single girl named Kate whom I had met in my Life Bible study class. She was struggling in her faith. She approached me about discipleship. She had been genuinely saved but had not continued to follow Christ in obedience. We began to meet weekly and focused on the plan I have laid out in this book. She seemed to be progressing, but then a romantic relationship began to claim her time. She met with me less and less and ultimately abandoned her daily time with the Lord. Shortly after, she and her new friend Thomas became engaged. Thomas was a young believer. He was excited about his new faith and was genuinely trying to follow Christ. Sadly, they had given in to temptation and become sexually involved. Their immorality began to trouble Thomas, but Kate was persuasive. Kate had become a stumbling block. He explained to her his need to abstain, but she continued to tempt him. He was being mentored by a friend in his men's group and was advised to break the engagement. She was devastated. She came to me, a weepy mess. She was focused on the embarrassment of telling her parents. She fretted about the money spent, the wasted dress, the printed invitations, and other related concerns.

I knew God wanted her attention. So we sat before the Lord together in prayer. God has the answers if we will simply stop and seek His counsel. If we will take the time to study His Word, usually we can avoid the drama that follows sin. In this case, I believed the Lord wanted her to seek her fiancé's forgiveness. After much remorse and admission of guilt for her part in their failure, she was ready to seek forgiveness. She went to him and confessed that she had been intentionally tempting him. She was genuinely contrite. Their relationship was restored, and they are a happily married Christian couple today with two children. They continue to serve the Lord and are raising their children to follow Christ as well.

This is just one example of how God's simple instruction and prayerful counsel can redeem what seems irrevocably broken.

It is my prayer that this little book will help you fall deeper in love with Him too, that it will lead you on the path to a richer, more fulfilling life.

Before we begin, however, as with anything, there must be a foundation. Putting in windows and sheetrock will do us little good if there is no foundation to our home. So, let's begin to build.

CHAPTER 2

FOUNDATION

For no one can lay any foundation other than the one already laid, which is Jesus Christ.
1 Corinthians 3:11

Friend, have you ever invited the Savior to save you? This is the foundation on which we build. As a young woman, I always wondered why Jesus had to die. I mean, what was the point? Yes, I had heard all my life that He died for my sins, but it escaped me! The truth was, I did not realize I was lost. I did not comprehend I needed someone to pay for my sins. I thought I could just be a good person, and eventually, magically, my good would outweigh my bad. This was bad theology. The truth was, I was separated from our holy God. I needed someone to bridge the gap for me. I needed someone to pay for the things that separated me from God. Of course, God knew this all along, and this is why He sent Jesus to pay the penalty. As the hymn proclaims, "He paid a debt He did not owe, I owed a debt I could not pay."[1] If you have invited Jesus Christ into your heart, the Holy Spirit resides with you, and

---

1   "He Paid a Debt He Did Not Owe," author unknown.

He will never leave you or forsake you. He has deposited the Holy Spirit who will guide you, teach you, comfort you, and intercede for you. That's God's promise.

When I was a student at the University of Kentucky, I remember coming in one night from "the" party with "the" guy. I still remember the feeling. It was an emptiness I hadn't noticed before. I remember thinking, "Is this all there is? Is this really one of the pinnacles of my life? Why do I feel so empty? What's missing?" Has this happened to you? Have you tried to fill your empty heart with things the world says are success? Or maybe worse, have you tried to fill it with mind-numbing drugs or alcohol? Perhaps you stuff your empty places with activities to keep you busy. Whatever your stuffing of choice, there is only one thing that will satisfy. Only your Creator God can fulfill your longing. Only He can fill the voids in your life.

A year or so after my empty experience in college, I was alone in my dorm. I was bored with studying and found all my friends were out. I discovered some girls in the hall who were from a local church. They had come to visit someone else who was not available. I invited them to sit with me, thinking I had found a distraction. At my invitation, they began to share with me how I could be forgiven for all my past, present, and future sins. They explained that I could become clean like a new baby. I only needed to invite Jesus into my empty heart and let Him fill the void. It was a free gift! What? How could it be that simple? Don't I need to do something? Don't I need to pay? I knew it had to cost something. And it did! But not to you and me. Salvation was a free gift? It just seemed too easy. When they asked if I'd like to invite Christ into my heart, I wasn't interested. Sadly, I rejected God's offer. I wasted a lot of time afterward chasing the wind. You can never get back wasted time. I urge you not to make the same mistake.

Eventually, as the Holy Spirit of God continued to call me, I stopped running. I wrongly thought that God was chasing me to take something away from me when, in reality, He was chasing me to give me something. That "something" was eternal life, peace, forgiveness, joy, and unconditional love. If you're still running from God, let me encourage you to stop. Let Him catch you. You'll never regret it.

Now, let's begin the journey to get off our couch. Let's begin a life-changing habit that will revolutionize our faith. We'll start with three questions.

CHAPTER 3

WHEN, WHERE, AND HOW?

Let us then approach God's throne of grace with
confidence, so that we may receive mercy and find
grace to help us in our time of need.
Hebrews 4:16

You may be thinking that spending quantity and quality time with God sounds overwhelming. When would I meet with Him? What would we talk about? How would I begin? Let's consider these questions.

WHEN?

First, when would you meet with the Lord? There is a principle in the Word of God called *first fruits.* It finds its origins in the Levitical law.[2] The Lord was calling His people to give Him their first fruits. The psalmist wrote, *The earth is the LORD's and everything in it, the world, and all who live in it; for he founded it upon the seas and established it upon the waters* (Psalm 24:1). Everything God's people had belonged to Him;

---

2   Leviticus 23:9-14

He was asking them to give back a portion. He was asking for their first and best. He still asks us today to give Him our best and our first. Usually, this refers to possessions and money, but have you considered that God expects us to tithe our time?

Many verses in Scripture refer to rising early in the morning to meet with the Lord. Psalm 119:147 says, *I rise before dawn and cry for help; I have put my hope in your word.* David wrote, *In the morning, LORD, you hear my voice; in the morning I lay my requests before you and wait expectantly* (Psalm 5:3).

This may seem impossible to you, and sometimes, in certain seasons of your life, it almost is. Maybe you simply begin by setting your alarm fifteen minutes earlier than usual. It's a great start. Perhaps some of your prayer time may need to be in the evening. But starting your day with the Lord will begin the transformation you and God are seeking. It will fuel your engine for the rest of the day. You will be able to ask the Lord how He wants you to spend your day. I have personally wasted way too much time spending my days aimlessly. Your life can bear no meaningful fruit without God's leading. If we aim at nothing, we will hit nothing.

Perhaps you have been spending time with the Lord in the mornings for years and you know the joy of sweet fellowship with Him. You have experienced life-changing principles that govern your life. You need no prompting to set aside special time with Him. That's great! What I am promoting in this book is a tool to make that intentional time all it can be. I'm sure many of you have a plan that is working. Hopefully, I will be sharing some helpful adjuncts to what you're already doing.

WHERE?

Where do I fellowship with the Lord? is the second question to answer. Certainly, where you meet with the Lord is not the most important thing. However, it is helpful to have a meeting place, a place that is set apart, sanctified for hallowed time with just Him. This should be a peaceful place, a place where you have some privacy and can expect to have few or no interruptions. It was said about Jesus: *Very early in the morning, while it was still dark, Jesus got up, left the house and went off to a solitary place, where he prayed* (Mark 1:35).

Consider your home. Is there a place that comes to mind? I have a study. It is away from the activities in our home, and I love it. In my previous homes, I used to love sitting at my kitchen table before the kids were up. I can remember a time when I had a nice-sized master closet. That was a great retreat for me. There I had precious times sitting at His feet, pouring out my heart and listening to Him speak. There is a meeting place in your home too.

I recommend getting organized ahead of time. Consider placing your study Bible, your journal, a pen, and notecards in a tote bag. This is simply a suggestion, but it is helpful to be prepared to meet with Him. Sometimes during these intimate conversations, you may have an impression; write it down for further meditation or deeper study later. It is also helpful

to plan against distractions. I put my phone out of my reach so that I won't be tempted to send that one important text or make that dental appointment. All of us are apt to lose our concentration. It has helped me to place a to-do notepad and pen close by. This way, if I have something I'm tempted to respond to immediately, I just jot down the reminder. I am generally able to move forward with my sacred time without jumping into my distraction.

HOW?

You have developed a place to meet with the Lord and a time to meet with Him. Now what? How do we enter the throne room of our holy God? Do we slide in on our knees? The answer is, sometimes. There are times in our lives when the emotions and hurts are so deep that we need comfort now. Our need is overwhelming, and we run to His side and throw ourselves in His lap. Our Abba Daddy God loves us. He knows when our hearts are broken and when nothing will do but a big hug from our Abba. But these should be the exception and not the rule. So how do we generally enter the throne room of God Almighty?

I believe that the Scriptures show us that we enter into the throne room with praise and thanksgiving. Psalm 100:4-5 says, *Enter his gates with thanksgiving and his courts with praise; give thanks to him and praise his name. For the LORD is good and his love endures forever; his faithfulness continues through all generations.*

We enter the throne room with reverence and awe. When the disciples asked Jesus to teach them to pray, Jesus gave them the "Lord's Prayer." It begins, *Our Father in heaven, hallowed be your name* (Matthew 6:9). Jesus is modeling for us how we enter the presence of our holy God.

It is crucial that we enter the presence of God in seclusion. I do not mean we have to be alone to pray, but the attitude of our hearts must be that there is no one else or anything else. Our focus and communication are with just Him. *But when you pray, go into your room, close the door and pray to your Father, who is unseen. Then your Father, who sees what is done in secret, will reward you* (Matthew 6:6). This alone time with Him is critical to our entering in. In his book, *Simply Prayer*, Bill Elliff described his idea of entering into God's presence.

Imagine opening a door and stepping into a foyer, the entrance to God's throne room. Now, turn behind you as you enter and shut the door. Shut the door on others and last week and next week. Even in a sense, shut the door on yourself. Your sole focus is the one you are about to encounter. Next, consciously step into the throne room of God! You have total access here because of Jesus Christ. Pause as you enter and look around. As you gaze throughout the Throne Room, you will see Christ seated at the right hand of the Father, and you will notice that He always lives to make intercession for His children. Angels hover around the throne. Praise is unending. Let the wonder of this environment overwhelm you. Your heart will begin to be filled with worship. Our God is Holy![3]

---

3   Bill Elliff, *Simply Prayer: Joining God for the Rest of Your Life*

When God gave His people instructions to build the temple, He was very specific. The measurements were precise, the materials precise. The Lord himself directed the layout and use. The Holy of Holies, the dwelling place of the Most High God, was to be protected by several outer areas. Only the High Priest could enter and only once a year to offer sacrifices for the sins of the people and himself. It was a picture of the majesty and awe due our glorious God. Tradition says the High Priest would tie a rope with bells around his ankle, a precaution in case he was struck dead for entering God's presence in an unworthy manner. His body could then be dragged from beneath the heavy curtain, protecting others from the same fate.

That's pretty serious! God is not mocked! He remains the Holy God Almighty! It is true that as believers we now have access to the King of Kings through the blood of Jesus, but we are still admonished to honor, praise, and worship God as holy. When I struggle with focus, I often find that a favorite praise and worship song helps center my mind and soul on our majestic King. *Our Father in heaven, hallowed be your name.* When we enter His throne room, let us remember where we are.

CHAPTER 4

ADORATION

Sing the praises of the LORD, you his faithful people; praise his holy name. For his anger lasts only a moment, but his favor lasts a lifetime; weeping may stay for the night, but rejoicing comes in the morning.
Psalm 30:4-5

PRAISING GOD FROM YOUR HEART

Praise is defined as "the act of expressing approval or admiration; commendation; laudation; the offering of grateful homage in words or song, as an act of worship: a hymn of praise to God."[4] According to the Oxford dictionary, worship is defined as "the offering of devotion, praise, and adoration to that which is deemed worthy of such offering, usually God."[5]

We can praise God for who He is. We can also praise God for what He does. There are subtle distinctions between these

---

4   *Dictionary.com*, s.v. "praise," accessed July 25, 2023, http://www.dictionary. com/browse/praiseful.
5   *Oxford Reference*, s.v. "worship," accessed July 25, 2023, https://www. oxfordreference.com/display/10.1093/acref/9780192800947.001.0001/ acref-9780192800947

two. We praise God as Creator God because that's who He is, but that's also what He does. So, who is this holy God? How do we praise and worship God Almighty?

Many years ago, when I was a young mother, God spoke to me while I was praying in my walk-in closet. I remember exactly my location and my posture. I remember it like it was yesterday. I heard the Lord say, "Wash my feet." I was so excited to obey Him. I said, "Oh, yes, Lord! What do you want me to do?"

I believed that when Jesus washed the disciples' feet, He was teaching them to serve one another. I said, "Lord, I am willing! What service do you want me to do?" For years, I served in teaching, I served in missions, I served with children, and for years, I asked the Lord, "Is this it?" I never sensed I had stumbled on the answer. It remained an unsettled wonder.

Fast forward many years later. I was in a prayer group and heard for the first time the song, "Jesus, We Love You." The chorus speaks of pouring out our love and reverence in the humblest way at Jesus' feet. Instantly, I knew! This was how I was to wash His feet. Just as Mary of Bethany chose to sit at His feet. And just as Mary the sinner chose to wash His feet with her tears, He wanted me to do the same.

He wanted my unbridled adoration. Mary's worship pleased Jesus. Martha, who chose to serve, had missed the best. *'Martha, Martha,' the Lord answered, 'you are worried and upset about many things, but few things are needed—or indeed only one. Mary has chosen what is better, and it will not be taken away from her'* (Luke 10:41-42).

A woman in that town who lived a sinful life learned that Jesus was eating at the Pharisee's house, so she came there with an alabaster jar of perfume. As she stood behind him at his feet weeping, she began to wet his feet with her tears. Then she wiped them with her hair, kissed them and poured perfume on them (Luke 7:37-38).

Adoration. This, friends, is worship! It is our greatest joy and privilege as children of the King. Worship can transport us instantly into the very presence of God where we can experience rest for our souls and peace for our troubled minds. Praise and worship are the keys to intimacy. Jesus told the Pharisees that if His disciples did not praise Him, the stones would cry out (Luke 19:40). Let's not allow the stones to cry out in our place.

Whom or what do I worship? This is a good question to ask ourselves. To whom or what am I devoting my time and energy? To what do I give my affection, my devotion? Whatever or whomever that is, that is whom or what I worship. Does this mean that because I work eight hours a day, I worship my work? No! But if it becomes my primary love, then yes, it's a form of worship. Let us intentionally praise and worship our worthy, perfect God!

A PRAYER OF PRAISE

Father God, it is a privilege to come before You as Your beloved child. Lord God Almighty, holy is Your name! I stand in awe of You, O God. I bow before You to worship and adore You. You alone are God; there is no other. Without You, I have no good thing. Holy is the name of the Lord! You are the air I breathe. You have rescued me from the pit and set my feet on a rock. Holy, holy is the name of the Lord.

Lord, You are Jehovah, God Almighty. Nothing is impossible for You. You are my Savior, saving me from destruction. You are the King of Kings and Lord of Lords. You are my hiding place, my strong tower. You are my refuge and strength. You alone are worthy to be praised. I bow in reverence before You. My heart is prostrate before You. My soul adores You. Praise Your mighty name!

Try making a list of praises to our God from your heart.

_____

_____

_____

_____

_____

PRAISING GOD THROUGH SCRIPTURE

Since you and I will be praising Him daily, there will be times when we just aren't able to think of anything inspiring to pray. That's okay! There are times when God has us in the wilderness and we feel dry as dust. During those times, we may be tempted to walk away from our commitment to meet regularly with Him. At first, we miss one day, then two, and before we know it, we are spending weeks without personal time with Him. We might say, "I don't feel anything." And it is exactly here, in this dry place, where we are tested. Can we obey God when we don't get our reward of joyous feelings? We say, "Lord, I put my money in the machine, now where's my candy bar? I spent time with You as I committed to do, yet I'm not experiencing joy. Where is my peaceful feeling? Where is my mountaintop?" Sometimes the truth is that we're in the valley. That's when we go back to what we have decided.

I decided to meet with God daily to build intimacy. The Word says in John 15:4, *Remain in me, as I also remain in you. No branch can bear fruit by itself; it must remain in the vine. Neither can you bear fruit unless you remain in me.* When the feelings aren't there, we dig in our heels and proclaim, "I will obey!"

God has called us into a love relationship, so in those lonely places, I often go to the Psalms. I've marked my Bible in the many places where David praised the Lord. David learned to praise our God even as a young shepherd boy, and his songs of praise are inspirational.

The Bible is full of worshipful monologues. Find the ones that speak to you. Consider researching the praises in Isaiah and other books of the Bible. Look at scriptures from the New Testament as well. Many passages speak of what God has done and of who He is to the church.

Try listing several psalms that speak of who God is and what He has done. Here are a few examples:

Who is God?

God is our refuge and strength, an ever-present help in trouble (Psalm 46:1).

_____

_____

_____

_____

_____

_____

What has God done for us?

For you created my inmost being; you knit me together in my mother's womb. I praise you because

I am fearfully and wonderfully made; your works are wonderful, I know that full well (Psalm 139:13-14).

_____

_____

_____

_____

_____

List praises from the New Testament.

What has God done for me?

It is for freedom that Christ has set us free. Stand firm, then, and do not let yourselves be burdened again by a yoke of slavery (Galatians 5:1).

_____

_____

_____

_____

_____

PRAYING WORSHIP SONGS

You may also want to think of worship songs that have blessed you and pray those lyrics back to God. Make a list of your favorite hymns and worship songs. Consider praying some of the more inspirational ones back to Him.

Here's an example from the hymn "Great is Thy Faithfulness."[6]

Almighty God, I praise You that You are faithful. Great is Thy faithfulness, O God my Father! There is no shadow of turning with Thee. I praise You that Thou changest not, that Thy compassions they fail not. As Thou hast been, Thou forever will be. Thank You, Father.

List your favorite Christian hymns that move you to worship our great God.

_____

_____

_____

_____

_____

_____

6   Thomas Chisholm, "Great Is Thy Faithfulness," Chicago: Hope,1923.

PRAISING GOD THROUGH HIS NAMES
AND HIS CHARACTER

It is always an uplifting experience for me to praise God by His names and titles. The Bible gives us many that describe His character or His works. Consider doing a personal study.

Who is God to you?

Example: God is my comforter.

_____

_____

_____

_____

_____

_____

What about His character draws you to His side?

He is unchanging. I can always count on Him to be the same God – yesterday, today, and forever.

_____

_____

_____

_____

_____

_____

What does He do that blesses your soul?

Who redeems your life from the pit and crowns you with love and compassion (Psalm 103:4).

_____

_____

_____

_____

If you're like me, those things are inexhaustible. I am forever grateful that He is "Savior." I never tire of worshiping and thanking Him for redeeming my lackluster life.

God is our refuge and strength, an ever-present help in trouble. Therefore we will not fear, though the earth give way and the mountains fall into the heart of the sea (Psalm 46:1-2).

Hallelujah! I never tire that He is my Refuge. I am so grateful that I can run to Him and find comfort in the refuge of His arms. Think about the characteristics that inspire you.

What's one of your favorite sacred qualities of our holy God?

Example: He is trustworthy.

_____

_____

_____

_____

_____

My personal favorite quality is His forgiving nature. What a miracle it is to have my sins blotted out. The Bible says He has removed my sin as far as the east is from the west (Psalm 103:12). How can that be? It seems too good to be true. I marvel at how He forgives my past, present, and future sins. Wow! Thank you, Lord! How could He overlook and excuse my disgusting trespasses? I don't understand, but I am so grateful! Thank you, Lord!

A few more examples to get you started:

Savior, Redeemer, King of Kings, The Great I Am, My Rock, Deliverer, Christ the Lord, Lamb of God, Strong Tower, My Shield, Shepherd, Master, Alpha and Omega, The Word, Light of the World, Wonderful Counselor

_____

_____

_____

_____

_____

_____

The many Hebrew names of God also can inspire our praise. I have listed a few for you below. You may enjoy researching these further.

ELOHIM My Creator
YAHWEH I Am
JEHOVAH My Lord God
EL SHADDAI My Supplier
ADONAI My Master
JEHOVAH JIREH My Provider
JEHOVAH ROPHE My Healer
JEHOVAH NISSI My Banner
JEHOVAH MAKADESH My Sanctifier
YAHWEH ROI My Shepherd
EL ROI The God Who Sees Me
EL KANNA Consuming Fire
YAHWEH TSURI My Rock
EL ELYON God Most High
BASILUS BASILEON King of Kings
MIGDAL-OZ Strong Tower
ISH Husband

_____

_____

_____

_____

_____

_____

David Jeremiah wrote, "Knowing God by His personal names is one of the greatest privileges for followers of Christ. The word *God* is found throughout the Bible, but the Lord reveals Himself more personally through the names with which He introduces Himself in Scripture. These names help us when we address Him in prayer. Just as we want to call people by the right term or name, so we want to address God with appropriate wisdom and reverence whenever we pray."[7]

Adoration and affection are essential to building a deep relationship with God Almighty. This time is sacred, set apart for just the two of you. *Our Father in heaven, hallowed be your name.* Praise and worship deposit us into the Holy of Holies. Could there be any greater honor or privilege?

---

7   David Jeremiah, "The Names of God and Why They Matter," DavidJeremiah. org, accessed July 1, 2023, http://www.davidjeremiah.org/knowgod/ the-names-of-god.

CHAPTER 5

THANKSGIVING

*Give thanks to the LORD, for he is good. His love
endures forever.*
Psalm 136:1

It is easy to confuse praising God and thanking God, but they are subtly different. We praise God for who He is and for what He does. We thank God for His gifts and blessings in our life.

Thankfulness is a muscle we need to strengthen. The spirit of gratitude must be exercised and developed. We don't always recognize that the gifts in our life come straight from God's hand. *Every good and perfect gift is from above, coming down from the Father of the heavenly lights, who does not change like shifting shadows* (James 1:17). Too often, we take these gifts for granted or we don't correctly attribute them to God. The truth is that ingratitude is a sin. Romans 1:21 states, *For although they knew God, they neither glorified him as God nor gave thanks to him.* Developing a spirit of gratitude is essential to our growth.

When God gives us a direct command, He requires our obedience to it, and He provides the power for us to obey. Many times the Bible commands us to thank God. It is true that we may not always feel thankful, but feelings are rarely our best gauge. Sometimes we must simply obey the directive. Often I have found that when I begrudgingly thank God for something I didn't want, in time, He supplies the feeling. For example, I have the gift of evangelism, and I have been praying for years for revival. I thrill at the invitation for lost souls to come to the altar. My heart swells as I see repentant souls giving their hearts to our Savior, no longer stumbling in the dark but coming to the light. So, when the worldwide coronavirus pandemic, hit our country and the whole world, I was naturally distressed. However, I sensed that the Lord expected me to thank Him for this unwanted intruder. It felt insincere as I obeyed His voice, but as I began to hear the stories of small pockets of revivals around the world, I rested. And as I observed frightened people looking up for the first time, I felt thankful.

> *Give thanks in all circumstances; for this is God's will for you in Christ Jesus.*
> (1 Thessalonians 5:18)

> *Praise the LORD. Give thanks to the LORD, for he is good; his love endures forever.*
> (Psalm 106:1)

> *Let the peace of Christ rule in your hearts, since as members of one body you were called to peace. And*

be thankful. Let the message of Christ dwell among you richly as you teach and admonish one another with all wisdom through psalms, hymns, and songs from the Spirit, singing to God with gratitude in your hearts. And whatever you do, whether in word or deed, do it all in the name of the Lord Jesus, giving thanks to God the Father through him.
(Colossians 3:15-17)

I will give thanks to you, LORD, with all my heart; I will tell of all your wonderful deeds. I will be glad and rejoice in you; I will sing the praises of your name, O Most High.
(Psalm 9:1-2)

THANKSGIVING LIST

As you begin to practice this directive, I have some suggestions. It has been very helpful for me to categorize my thanksgiving list. When we organize our thoughts and prepare, we will be more thorough in whatever we do. Your categories will likely be different from mine. Usually, I begin by thanking Him for something regarding my husband. For example, I may thank our God for my husband's recent healthy doctor's report. There are unlimited things we can be grateful for regarding our spouse. We may be thankful for his peaceful workplace. We may be thankful for his thoughtful supervisor. Being intentional and specific about your appreciation for God's provision will help you develop joy and contentment.

Gratitude for something specific about our children would be a high priority on my list. My son has a lovely family. His wife is precious. His children overwhelm me with joy and contentment. He is very successful in his profession. He loves his father and me. I am so grateful! My daughter has recently married an amazing godly man whom I adore. She has a good mind, earned a bachelor's degree from the University of Alabama, and is enjoying many adventures. She is excited about her new life. She loves her father and me. I am so grateful!

Then, I may thank God for someone in my family of origin. My mother turned 92 this past June. Her good health and good mind are such a blessing to my family. She actually flew by herself (with the help of the airline attendants) from our hometown in Kentucky to my home in Houston, Texas. We had two lovely weeks together. We drove twice to our beach house, which she loved. We ate at some of Galveston's best restaurants. We sat on the balcony overlooking the ocean and visited for hours. She asked to walk on the beach, and with my husband's help, she waded in the water and felt the sand squish beneath her feet. She had such a great time. I can't tell you how grateful I am that she and I could share those weeks together.

I thank my God every time I remember you.
(Philippians 1:3)

My list would include someone or something at work. For example, I may be grateful for my profession, for the satisfaction I receive from my work. I may be grateful for my coworkers and pleasant work environment. My list may include my income, my benefits package, or my flexible hours. There are many things we can be grateful for regarding our work. Employment is a privilege. Many countries do not provide the opportunities Americans enjoy. My husband is an entrepreneur. I appreciate his passion to produce. He is fulfilled in his profession. I am thankful!

My gratitude list may include a neighbor, a church member, and as you can see, the list can be as long or short as you want. Categorizing helps me to recall things or people I would not always remember. It causes me to focus and encourages me to organize my thoughts. It's a method that may or may not work for you, but I hope you will give it a try.

Examples: Spouse, Son, Daughter, Brother/sister/ parents, Work, Church, Something material, Something physical, Friends/neighbors, Your country/ leaders, Answered prayers

_____

_____

_____

_____

_____

GRATITUDE JOURNAL

Another useful tool I've found that helps me obey God in regard to thanksgiving is a gratitude journal. This may also include categories, or it may be set up as journaling the things you appreciate about your husband, your daughter, your son, and whomever or whatever you choose. Maybe you would like to make an ongoing list of things you're grateful for about your church. You may want to include your pastor and his wife. You might choose to include a small study group you particularly love. Personally, I am grateful for the ministry opportunities my church has provided throughout the years. Your gratitude journal is personal and can include anything for which you'd like to thank our great God. Taking the time to develop a gratitude journal will help you accomplish our mission of expressing our thankfulness and building intimacy with the Lord.

One of the other reasons I practice thanksgiving is that it literally creates in me a joyful heart. It helps me control fearful thoughts. It refocuses my mind. When I review with God His endless gifts, I find I am more content. I am filled with joy and genuinely grateful! God does not need my gratitude, but He knows how it blesses me to have a grateful heart.

Thankfulness redirects my anxious thoughts. I find I can be content in my circumstances. It helps me put things in perspective. It helps me to see things are not really that bad. Our emotions will deceive us if we listen to them. They will cause us to unravel. Emotions are liars. They will take us places we don't want to go. They will make us do and say things we don't want to do or say. If we do not discipline them through the Holy Spirit who indwells us, we will sin. But if we practice the spirit of gratitude, it will bring us back to what is real.

Rejoice always, pray continually, give thanks in all circumstances; for this is God's will for you in Christ Jesus (1 Thessalonians 5:16-18).

I had breast cancer 10 years ago. The fear associated with it threatened to rob me of any peace or joy. The dread and oppression of just walking into the oncology department was palpable. However, God had been teaching me about controlling my thoughts. He had been speaking to me about joy and gratitude in the face of circumstances. I clearly remember, as an absolute act of the will, saying over and over, "I choose to trust you, God. I choose to be at peace. I choose to be content. I choose to thank you in the dark." It calmed my anxious heart and centered my thoughts on the truth: God is in control. Thanking God in the dark is unnatural. I sure didn't feel thankful for cancer. But there is power in obeying God.

He lifted me out of the slimy pit, out of the mud and mire; he set my feet on a rock and gave me a firm place to stand (Psalm 40:2).

Yours, LORD, is the kingdom; you are exalted as head over all. Wealth and honor come from you; you are the ruler of all things. In your hands are strength and power to exalt and give strength to all. Now, our God, we give you thanks, and praise your glorious name (1 Chronicles 29:11-13).

Communicating thankfulness is critical in our relationships. It is particularly crucial when it is directed at our great God. Expressing gratitude to the Lord helps us create intimacy. Taking the time to appreciate and express our blessings and appreciation opens the door to fellowship with our Creator. A psalm many of us learned as children expresses this well:

Shout for joy to the LORD, all the earth. Worship the LORD with gladness; come before him with joyful songs. Know that the LORD is God. It is he who made us, and we are his; we are his people, the sheep of his pasture. Enter his gates with thanksgiving and his courts with praise; give thanks to him and praise his name. For the LORD is good and his love endures forever; his faithfulness continues through all generations (Psalm 100).

CHAPTER 6

CONFESSION AND REPENTANCE

Whoever conceals their sins does not prosper, but the one who confesses and renounces them finds mercy.
Proverbs 28:13

Speaking of confession, I must confess that this is my least favorite part of my daily prayer time. Thinking of my transgressions against God and others is unpleasant. I'd rather skip it. But I know the folly of not laying my transgressions before God for His miraculous mercy. I know the foolhardiness of holding on to a guilty conscience. A heavy heart will weigh us down with burdens that are too heavy to carry. We weren't meant to live with downcast souls. We are required to confess and repent. In the Garden of Eden, when Cain brought his less-than-acceptable offering to the Lord, we see the picture of our forgiving God's heart. *Then the LORD said to Cain, 'Why are you angry? Why is your face downcast? If you do what is right, will you not be accepted? But if you do not do what is right, sin is crouching at your door; it desires to have you, but you must rule over it'* (Genesis 4:6-7). The

Lord wants to save us from ourselves. He wants to spare us from heavy hearts.

A happy heart makes the face cheerful, but heartache crushes the spirit (Proverbs 15:13).

SINS AGAINST GOD

Psalm 139:23-24 says, *Search me, God, and know my heart; test me and know my anxious thoughts. See if there is any offensive way in me, and lead me in the way everlasting.*

I like to think of this as God holding a flashlight into my soul. Light invades darkness, and it cannot stand. God is the Light of the world. Light will always overcome the darkness. Our souls crave light and purity. It is critical that we cleanse our conscience of guilt. Guilt weighs us down. We feel heavy, we feel burdened. Guilt will make us sick. The Word of God says, *If we confess our sins, he is faithful and just and will forgive us our sins and purify us from all unrighteousness* (1 John 1:9). What a great promise! I love feeling clean. You know how it feels when you have been on a camping trip or a hiking trip or even a long plane ride? Showering can literally wash away our stress. Clean feels good! Being clean in our souls feels even better.

SINS AGAINST OTHERS

'Teacher, which is the greatest commandment in the Law?' Jesus replied: 'Love the Lord your God with

all your heart and with all your soul and with all your mind.' This is the first and greatest commandment. And the second is like it: 'Love your neighbor as yourself' (Matthew 22:36-39).

Sinning against others is sadly a part of our human condition. We don't naturally want to love others as ourselves. We tend to love ourselves more. However, our great God requires us to truly love others. It is not natural. Sadly, it is natural to love oneself. Many of the sins we need to confess are centered around this very commandment. When we shine the flashlight into our hearts, we can see how we sin against others daily.

Recently, I visited a boutique in a shopping mall. I was in a hurry and wanted to find something to wear out of the store for dinner. I was in the dressing room when a salesgirl asked me to leave. I was instantly annoyed. I wasn't finished trying on my last-minute dinner clothes. I still needed something to wear. She said, "We are closing the dressing rooms. You need to leave now." Normally, I may not have been so aggravated, but I was in a hurry and grumpy. No excuses. I was rude to her. I was condescending. It wasn't pretty. I left angrily. Later, I discovered that she wanted me to leave because I had missed a sign saying, "Dressing rooms are closed for social distancing." Well, I was deeply troubled by this. Not only had I acted poorly, but I did this in front of my daughter-in-law. I felt so ashamed. Why was I so rude and arrogant? My soul was distressed within me. I knew God was definitely displeased with my behavior. I had some decisions to make. I could just confess my sin alone with

God and ask Him to forgive me, which I did immediately, or I could try to make this right with the offended parties as well.

First thing in the morning, I wrote a heartfelt apology to my daughter-in-law, asking her forgiveness for subjecting her to my embarrassing and rude behavior. She was gracious and replied, "No need to apologize," but I knew what I needed to do. Next, I went to a lovely store in the mall and had designer chocolates gift-wrapped. I wrote a note asking the salesclerk to forgive my arrogant and rude behavior. Then came the really hard part: I went to the store and asked for her. I don't think she recognized me, but I faced her and told her I was sorry for my rude behavior. I asked her to forgive me. She was immediately accepting and kind. I was forgiven! The burden left me. Confession and repentance cleanse us. I don't personally like the process, but I can't deny the results. Reconciliation with someone we have offended is gratifying.

> *Submit yourselves, then, to God. Resist the devil, and he will flee from you. Come near to God and he will come near to you. Wash your hands, you sinners, and purify your hearts, you double-minded. Grieve, mourn and wail. Change your laughter to mourning and your joy to gloom. Humble yourselves before the Lord, and he will lift you up* (James 4:7-10).

When you have been married as long as I have, you comprehend the importance of reconciliation. Living with bitterness, anger, and unforgiveness is a miserable state for anyone, especially in marriage where there is no opportunity to walk away. At the altar, we make a vow before our families and friends. We make a vow to one another. But marriage was designed by God, so, more importantly, we make a vow to God. Marriage is more than a promise; it is a covenant relationship. If people genuinely believed the Word of God, there would be no divorce. God does not make allowances for divorce, except in the case of adultery. Obviously, there are circumstances that involve self-preservation. Domestic violence is real, and so it is debated if it is a legitimate justification for divorce. Our great God is a reasonable judge. However, as a rule, there is no scriptural basis for divorce.

So where does that leave us when our spouses offend us? Where does that leave us when our love has grown cold or resentment and anger have choked our passion and joy? We have choices to make. We can give ourselves permission to add more bricks to the walls we have built, or we can decide to forgive and love. Yes, love is a decision. It is an action. Feelings are fickle. They cannot be trusted. The Word of God says, *Let the wife see that she respects and reverences her husband* [*that she notices him, regards him, honors him, prefers him, venerates, and esteems him; and that she defers to him, praises him, and loves and admires him exceedingly*] (Ephesians 5:33 AMPC). Again, if God has given us a directive to follow, He will give us the power to fulfill it.

Proverbs 14:1 says, *The wise woman builds her house, but with her own hands the foolish one tears hers down.*

God forgive us! We withhold affection. We retreat. We seek revenge. I am certain God shakes His holy head in sadness as we seek to crush the lives out of our own marriages.

I'm sure you are familiar with the much quoted "love chapter," 1 Corinthians 13. It's lovely. But when the Holy Spirit revealed to me that I needed to literally apply this to my marriage, I was troubled. The love God describes is agape love. Within Christianity, agape is considered to be the love originating from God and Christ for humankind. How can I love my husband the way God loves? I was especially troubled by the verse that said love is not easily offended or provoked. Frankly, my husband sometimes provokes me. He steps over my personal boundaries. Honestly, he has offended me a time or two in these last 38 years. If I were to obey God in this, I would need to learn to give my husband grace and let it go. I would need to give up some of my perceived rights to be angry, to stew, to shut down.

> *Fools show their annoyance at once, but the prudent overlook an insult* (Proverbs 12:16).

If we can truly overlook an insult, we will not build walls that separate. God inspired me to envision grace as being like plastic chips that I carried in my pocket. They were little invisible, personal gifts I could give my husband. And when I was offended, I would think, "I should gift him with a grace chip." After all, grace, which is undeserved favor, is what saved us sinners from hell. *For it is by grace you have been saved, through faith—and this is not from yourselves, it is the gift of God* (Ephesians 2:8).

It may sound silly, but this works. God expects us to give others "undeserved favor chips" just as He offers it to us. *Blessed are the merciful, for they will be shown mercy* (Matthew 5:7). For the same mercy you give is the same mercy you will receive. Personally, I want mercy. I need mercy. Let me be a person who freely gives it to others. Let me be a woman who builds her house, not the foolish one who tears it down with her own hands.

Now I know you are thinking, "Do you always do this?" The answer is a resounding "No!" I fail all the time. The answer to failure is, "Don't give up." When we trip over our own lips, we just need to reset. Say to yourself, "I can do better than that." It helps me! Maybe it will help you too. Remember, what is your end goal? Is it to win a fight? To be right? When we win a fight or prove we are right, we don't really win much, do we?

The other concept I always found troubling is that love keeps no record of wrongs (1 Corinthians 13:5). I find this particularly difficult. When my husband repeats an offense that we have often discussed, I am instantly angry. My mind says, "You just did this last week, and now I'm supposed to overlook it again? No way, buster! You're going to pay this time." The problem is that God said to overlook! He makes no mistakes. So what do we do with this? He expects us to give grace over and over. *Then Peter came to Jesus and asked, "Lord, how many times shall I forgive my brother or sister who sins against me?*

Up to seven times?" Jesus answered, "I tell you, not seven times, but seventy-seven times (Matthew 18:21-22). Surely, He didn't mean in marriage too? Rick Warren, writing about forgiveness in marriage said:

He [Jesus] is saying you have to just keep on doing it. You just keep on forgiving until the pain stops. Every time you remember that hurt, you make an intentional choice to say, 'God, that person really hurt me, and it still hurts. But because I want to be filled with love and not resentment, I am choosing to give up my right to get even and wish bad on that person. I am choosing to bless those who hurt me. God, I pray you'll bless their life – not because they deserve it. They don't. I don't deserve your blessing either, God. But I pray that you'd show grace to them like you've shown to me.'

It's not easy. In fact, I have no doubt that for some reading this, your marriage is about to self-destruct – not because of the hurt, but because of the unforgiveness. It's not the hurt but the refusal to forgive that destroys a marriage.

You may say, 'I don't feel like forgiving.' Who does? Nobody ever *feels* like forgiving. You do it because it's the right thing to do, and you do it to get on with your life. These steps are not easy, but with God's power, you can do it.[8]

I know this is difficult, but I promise you, it works! Keep giving that undeserved grace. It will pay big dividends. Walls come

---

8   Rick Warren, "How Often Should You Forgive?" PastorRick.com, July 14, 2017, https://pastorrick.com/devotional/

down. Trust is restored. The offending partner may change, but even if they don't, we can lay the offense at Christ's feet. We can rest in the truth that His ways are always right and that we can trust Him with the outcome.

1 Corinthians 13:4-7 says, *Love is patient, love is kind. It does not envy, it does not boast, it is not proud. It does not dishonor others, it is not self-seeking, it is not easily angered, it keeps no record of wrongs. Love does not delight in evil but rejoices with the truth. It always protects, always trusts, always hopes, always perseveres.*

Forgiveness is the best gift I've ever received. The *best*! I remember clearly the day after I invited Christ to invade my life. I was so relieved! I remember the clean, bright, ecstatic way I felt. I was brand new. No more guilt, no more shame. Free in an instant. We are designed to forgive. We are made in His image. He commands us to forgive. If it were not possible, He would never have commanded us to do it. We can lay it down. We have Holy Spirit power within us. *I can do all this through him who gives me strength* (Philippians 4:13). We have the same power that raised Jesus Christ from the dead. Glory!

Is there anyone in your life that you need to forgive? Think of family members, work associates, neighbors that you need to release from the prison you have built for them. The truth is, they often don't even know they are being held in contempt by us. We often seem to be the only ones suffering resentment, bitterness, and anger. Usually, the offending party has

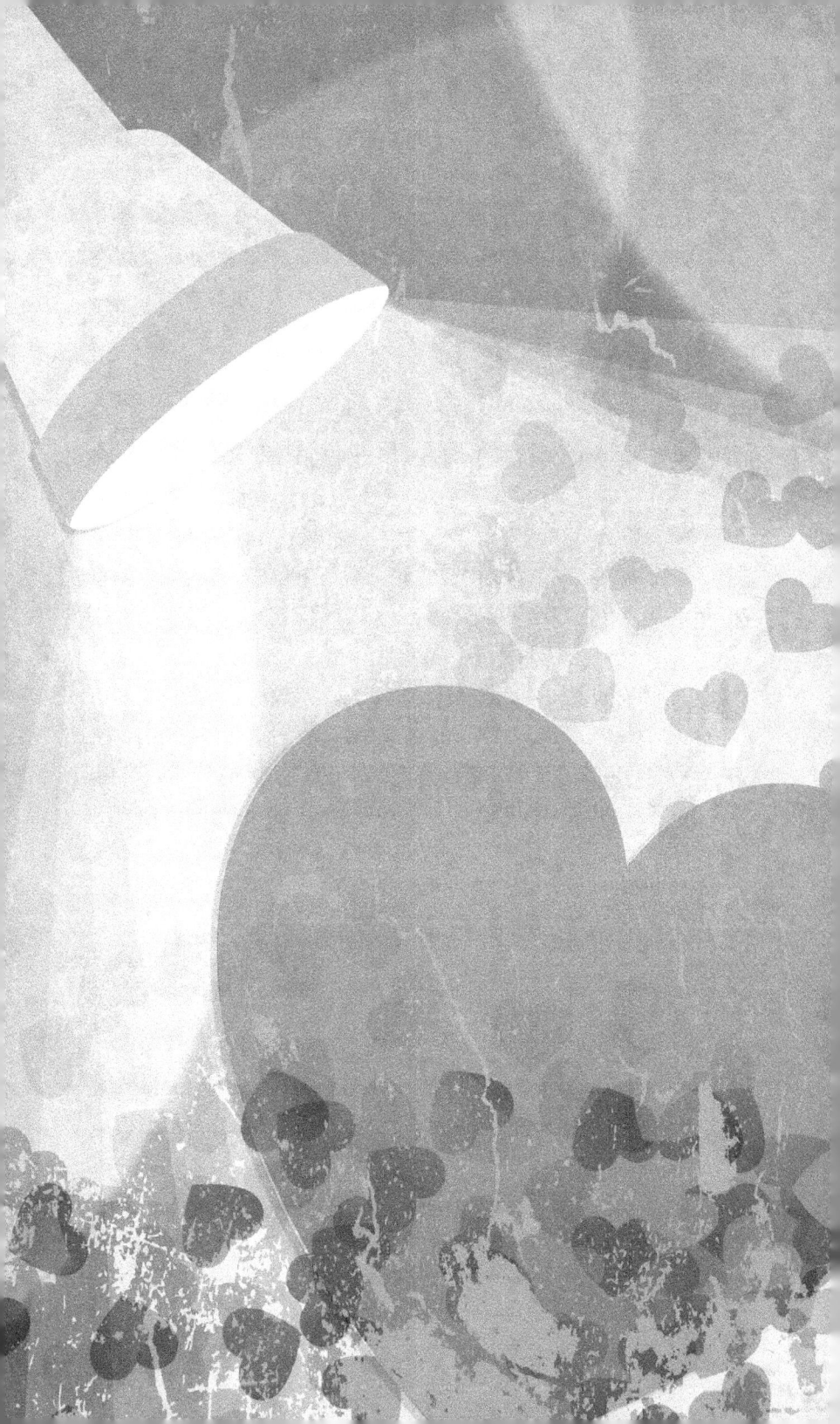

long forgotten about us. So, let's do ourselves a favor and let them go. Besides all this, our God commands it.

Bear with each other and forgive one another if any of you has a grievance against someone. Forgive as the Lord forgave you (Colossians 3:13).

Confession is critical to a successful relationship with God. We humans have found many ways to sin against God and others.

In your sacred time with the Lord, you may want to write down categories to remind you of sin you have repressed. Your categories may include:

SINS OF WRONG ATTITUDES AND THOUGHTS

Have we had angry, envious, or resentful thoughts? What about condescending, disrespectful, hostile, or vengeful thoughts?

For as he thinketh in his heart, so is he.
(Proverbs 23:7a KJV)

SINS IN RELATIONSHIPS

Whom have we wounded? Whom do we hold in contempt? Whom have we not forgiven?

For if you forgive other people when they sin against you, your heavenly Father will also forgive you. But if

*you do not forgive others their sins, your Father will
not forgive your sins.*
(Matthew 6: 14-15)

*For Moses said, 'Honor your father and mother,' and,
'Anyone who curses their father or mother is to be put
to death.'*
(Mark 7:10)

God is serious about sin. Let's keep a short record with Him.
Let's confess immediately as if we touched a hot stove.

Have we sinned this week against our spouse or our children? Against our parents or siblings? Friends, co-workers,
or neighbors?

SINS AGAINST GOD

*How much more severely do you think someone
deserves to be punished who has trampled the Son
of God underfoot, who has treated as an unholy thing
the blood of the covenant that sanctified them, and
who has insulted the Spirit of grace?*
(Hebrews 10:29)

Neglect

Have we given God our time and devotion this week? Did we
sit at His feet listening to His still small voice, or did we breeze
by Him on our way out the door?

Disobedience

Have we done anything this week that we know displeased God?

Rebellion

Have we dug in our heels? Have we allowed pride or stubbornness to win a battle or two this week?

Idolatry

Have we made something a priority above God? Has our time energy and devotion been misplaced this week?

> 'I am the LORD your God. . . . You shall have no other gods before me.'
> (Exodus 20:2-3)

Taking God's name in vain

Have we carelessly in our mind or with our lips used His name pointlessly?

Not keeping His Sabbath

Are we skipping church? Are we honoring our God on His holy day?

Do we spend His day on *self*?

SINS OF THE FLESH

The acts of the flesh are obvious: sexual immorality, impurity and debauchery; idolatry and witchcraft; hatred, discord, jealousy, fits of rage, selfish ambition, dissensions, factions and envy; drunkenness, orgies, and the like. I warn you, as I did before, that those who live like this will not inherit the kingdom of God.
(Galatians 5:19-21)

I am certain we did not cover all of the ways in which we can sin. I am grateful for a forgiving God who washes away our transgressions and then forgets about them. Praise God! We are free from the bondage of sin if we will simply confess, repent, and then forget. This is only possible in the Spirit. Our flesh cannot fulfill God's Word. Only the Holy Spirit within can do all things through Christ who strengthens us.

Cleansing our souls of the dirt we've collected throughout the day will release us from the bonds of guilt. We serve a forgiving God. Let us search the recesses of our hearts and confess anything we believe would displease Him and repent, turn from our sin. Confession is good for the soul; it is also commanded in God's Word.

In the past God overlooked such ignorance, but now he commands all people everywhere to repent.
(Acts 17:30)

CHAPTER 7

SUPPLICATION

Do not be anxious about anything, but in every situation, by prayer and petition, with thanksgiving, present your requests to God.

Philippians 4:6

Supplication is the action of asking or begging for something earnestly or humbly.[9] Requests, asking, supplicating – do you ask God? Do you sometimes feel that God is too busy for your silly problems? Do you keep them to yourself? Do you think, "This is too small to bother God with; I'll just handle it myself?" The thing is, our great God cares about everything that troubles us. His admonition is to pray about everything. I confess I do not always do this myself. I often try to solve my own problems. For example, I have an annoying, habitual, and endless problem: I lose everything! It's one of the great frustrations of my life. It is so aggravating; I really can't explain it. If there is someone in your family who has this malady, have a little mercy. It's much harder on us than it is

---

9   *Oxford Reference*, s.v. "supplication," accessed July 25, 2023, https://www.oxfordreference.com/display/10.1093/acref/9780199571123.001.0001/acref-9780199571123.

on you. Too frequently to recount, I will say to my husband, "Can you please help me find my keys, my purse, my jacket," and the list goes on. He will invariably say the same thing: "Have you asked the Lord where it is?" It's funny, but when I do stop to ask the Lord, He often reminds me where I've left it. It's not one hundred percent of the time, but usually! How foolish of me to tear through the house in desperate search when I could just relax and ask God. He loves us so much. He cares about every little thing we care about. He cares about the sparrow that falls, and He knows every hair on our head. We are cherished! Our Father loves His children. *Let your requests be made known to God.*

It may be hard for many of us to ask God about every little thing, but it is the common experience of the Christian to ask God for help. Often that is the centerpiece of our prayer life. We want to unburden ourselves at His feet. Sometimes, it's clear to us what we need to pray. Our burdens are obvious, and our troubles are heavy. During those times, there is no other place we'd rather be than on our knees. There is no better place to lighten our load.

> *'Come to me, all you who are weary and burdened, and I will give you rest. Take my yoke upon you and learn from me, for I am gentle and humble in heart, and you will find rest for your souls. For my yoke is easy and my burden is light'* (Matthew 11:28-30).

What a great promise. Hopefully, for most of us, our usual experience is not heavy burdens. Hopefully, our usual daily prayer will be ordinary, not full of angst. It is this daily prayer that I'd like to address. If you are a person who just can't think of what to pray about every single day, then you may want a plan. Sometimes I walk away from my prayers and think, "How could I have forgotten to ask about such and such?" If this is you, it may help to categorize your requests. For example, what do I need to pray about regarding my home? Are there any situations at work that I need to pray about? Perhaps friends, church, or my personal health. Maybe I need to request help with a personality weakness? For example, maybe I am short-tempered, easily offended, or impulsive. These weaknesses can affect our effectiveness in life. Our God wants to help us recognize these shortcomings and help us control them.

Personally, I need God's help with diligence. This is a common prayer for me. Unfortunately, I'm not as disciplined as I would like. Discipline and diligence are qualities I need to request often. I love sugar! Saying "no" to fudge just seems impossible. Currently, I am once again coming to the Lord with another failed diet. I was one of the lucky ones when I was young. I was always thin and ate whatever I wanted. My husband threatened to buy a T-shirt that said, "Give me your chocolate and no one will get hurt." I foolishly assumed this lovely gift of a crazy metabolism would last forever. Well, the party suddenly halted in my fifties. Now it was time to scramble and figure out how to exercise self-control in an area I formerly dismissed. Or, more importantly, I needed to learn how to eat healthily. Staying on track with a healthy diet is just so frustrating. This may not be your area, but for me,

I need help. I need God's strength. I need God's direction, training, and vision. I need Him! This is supplication, friend. We need divine help.

Supplication seems to be primarily requests for ourselves. Intercession is when we pray for others. This may sound self-serving, but truly it is essential. If I neglect to pray for myself, I become a target for the Enemy. I have not guarded myself against the fiery darts of the Evil One.

Therefore put on the full armor of God, so that when the day of evil comes, you may be able to stand your ground, and after you have done everything, to stand. Stand firm then, with the belt of truth buckled around your waist, with the breastplate of righteousness in place, and with your feet fitted with the readiness that comes from the gospel of peace. In addition to all this, take up the shield of faith, with which you can extinguish all the flaming arrows of the evil one. Take the helmet of salvation and the sword of the Spirit, which is the word of God. (Ephesians 6:13-17)

Here's the truth: If I have not put on my armor, I am moving through my day in the flesh. I need prayer. I need God to protect me from myself. I need resurrection power to proclaim the truths God has given me. How foolish of me to move into God's plans without consulting Him.

The Israelites sampled their provisions but did not inquire of the LORD (Joshua 9:14).

But when you pray, go into your room, close the door and pray to your Father, who is unseen. Then your Father, who sees what is done in secret, will reward you (Matthew 6:6).

In Gethsemane, Jesus prayed for Himself: *May this cup be taken from me* (Matthew 26:39).

You may ask, "What shall I pray for myself?" Here are some suggestions:

Pray for the armor of God.
Pray for wisdom.
Pray for strength.
Pray for peace.
Pray for direction.
Pray for diligence.
Pray for revelation.
Pray for spiritual gifts.
Pray as if it all depends on you, knowing it all depends on Him.

What keeps you up at night? What worry or worries try to get your attention? What thoughts try to steal your peace? Whatever that is, pray! Hannah Whitall Smith recalled talking to a visitor one day who said, "We must take our troubles to the Lord." "Yes," replied Hannah, "but we must do more than that. We must leave them there. Most people," she continued, "take their burdens to Him, but they bring them away with them again and are just as worried and unhappy as ever. But I take mine and leave them with Him and come away and forget them. If the worry comes back, I take it to Him again. I do this over and over, until at last I just forget I have any worries and am at perfect rest."[10] God wants our burdens. It is actually His desire to carry them for us.

Romans 8:26-27 says, *In the same way, the Spirit helps us in our weakness. We do not know what we ought to pray for, but the Spirit Himself intercedes for us through wordless groans. And he who searches our hearts knows the mind of the Spirit, because the Spirit intercedes for God's people in accordance with the will of God.*

Author Linda Dillow wrote, "Ask Him to take you deeper in all He is as Father, all He is as Son, and all He is as Spirit. Ask Him to teach you how to deeply worship Him. You know how to serve Him but He longs for you to slow down and be still and know that He is God. Crawl into His lap and breathe in His fragrance and sense His deep love for you. Stop. Be still. Listen. He longs for you to hear His personal voice to you."[11]

---

10   Hannah Whitall Smith, *The Christian's Secret to a Happy Life*, (New York: Fleming H. Revell, 1888).

11   Linda Dillow, "Q & A with Linda Dillow," Going Beyond Ministries, June 3, 2020, https://goingbeyond.com/blog/q-a-with-linda-dillow/.

CHAPTER 8

INTERCESSION

As for me, far be it from me that I should sin against the LORD by failing to pray for you. And I will teach you the way that is good and right.
1 Samuel 12:23

I remember the first time my mind registered this verse. It really caused me to pause. Am I actually sinning against God by not praying for others? This is staggering. We are commissioned to pray for others. It is our holy assignment. I need to remember to pray for others. I need to store their prayer requests, spoken and unspoken. If my friend is sick, clearly, I need to pray. If my family member is struggling with their faith, I need to pray. If my friend has lost their spouse, I am obliged to pray. This sounds obvious to those who have been following Christ for years, but I'm guessing even they could use reminders. How can we routinely pray for the needs and requests of those God has placed in our lives? Let's explore some methods that have worked for others.

I urge, then, first of all, that petitions, prayers, intercession and thanksgiving be made for all people.
(1 Timothy 2:1)

But I tell you, love your enemies and pray for those who persecute you.
(Matthew 5:44)

These verses are pretty convicting! Praying earnestly for others sounds like a huge responsibility and a daunting task, and frankly, it is. Praying for those who despitefully use you – now that's hard! Do we pray for those we feel have wronged us? It is one thing to release someone who has hurt us from the prison of unforgiveness. It is quite another to actually pray good things for them. I find that I fail in this more than I succeed. This kind of obedience takes focused intentionality on our part. Can we pray good things for these offenders? Can we obey God in this kind of intercession?

Are we diligently praying for our family and friends? It can be difficult to labor in prayer over our adult children's marriages, jobs, finances, or whatever burdens them. It is a heavy load to carry a friend through the loss of a loved one. And how many of us have watched our spouses shake their weary heads? Are we providing the prayer cover they need? Are we diligent in holding up their arms as they navigate the curves life throws at them? I know I have been guilty at times of serving and praying for everyone else, leaving my poor husband to fend for himself. Oh, how I hate to think of it. How dare I *not* hold my husband up when he's weary! Sometimes we mistakenly believe that our spouses are so strong that they are fortified by their own prayers. But how would I feel if my husband was not covering me with God's cloak of protection? It is truly a shameful thing to forget him. Praise God we have a Savior who forgives us when we are negligent and thoughtless.

> *Come to me, all you who are weary and burdened, and I will give you rest. Take my yoke upon you and learn from me, for I am gentle and humble in heart, and you will find rest for your souls. For my yoke is easy and my burden is light* (Matthew 11:28-30).

There is no doubt that God is serious about His directive for us to pray for others. So, how do we accomplish this command? Is this to be a tack-on to our prayers? Is this to be an impromptu, as-we-think-of-it prayer?

Sometimes our prayers for others are impromptu. The Spirit brings people to mind, and it is our privilege to lift these people up to our great God when we are prompted by the Holy Spirit. However, what I am suggesting is a more systematic and consistent plan – a way we can recall the needs of our friends and family members regularly.

Since you have begun to journal your praise, thanksgiving, confession, and supplication, you might add a section in the back for intercession.

Frankly, if I don't write it down, I often forget. So, I have a page just for my husband's needs and requests, and I have a page for each of my children. I often update these pages, adding current concerns.

Then in my intercession section in my journal, I have five columns. One for the *sick*, one for the *lost* (those who need Christ's gift of salvation), one for the *grieving and those who seem to be struggling with their faith*, one for the *lonely* (widows, singles, or whomever God brings to mind), and one for those with *financial or work-related needs*.

Going down each column, I insert the day of the week in which I plan to pray for these personal needs. I write the names in the column that fit that person's current need. For example, I may have a cousin who has just received a diagnosis that will require medical treatment. I will write his name in the "sick" column. So, on Mondays, I may pray for four people who are sick, maybe three who are grieving, and so on. This enables me to pray for each person at least once a week.

As you can see, your lists can be inexhaustible. These are only suggestions. You may have more or fewer columns. But the point is to remind yourself of the needs of those God has placed in your path.

You may also consider making a page for government officials and a section for your church staff, such as your pastor, associate pastor, and youth minister.

On the next page is an example of how you may potentially organize your intercession. I repeat, this is just a suggestion. You may have a better plan that works for you.

	Sick	Unbelievers
M.	Tommy	Laura
T.	Mary	Katherine
W.	Jack	Mark
T.	Amber	Michael
F.	Kevin	Danielle
	Grieving	**Lonely**
M.	Susan	Jeff
T.	Ms. Sands	Heather
W.	Ben	James
T.	Kelly	George
F.	Jamie	Jake
	Leaders	**Struggling**
M.	Government officials	Clara
T.	Church leadership	John
W.	School leadership	Angela
T.	Work leadership	Jordan
F.	City leadership	Abigail

Husband	Parents
Walk with God	Walk with God
Leadership	Health
Friendships	Wisdom
Workplace	Protection
Health	Church
Son	**Daughter**
Spiritual Growth	Faithfulness to God
Education	Career
Relationships	Friends
Time Management	Protection
Future Spouse	Children

Your categories may be different; they are simply meant to remind us to pray for these individuals at least once a week. You may be a person who remembers these needs without prompts, but I think most of us could use a system to prod us. Hopefully, this will inspire you to develop your own method.

Praying for others is a discipline that cannot be ignored. It is easy to overlook this important responsibility. But keep in mind how dependent we have been on other's prayers. We have each faced our own giants. When we are so burdened we can hardly pray for ourselves, what a comfort to know that others are kneeling, fasting, and petitioning God on our behalf. Let us stay committed to lifting our loved ones up to the throne of the only One who can meet their needs and carry their burdens. Let us remain faithful.

CHAPTER 9

SURRENDER. REST IS POSSIBLE

Trust in the LORD with all your heart and lean not on your own understanding.
Proverbs 3:5

Feelings can be wonderful, or feelings can be a nightmare. They are powerful. They can lead us where we don't want to go. They can throw us into turmoil and confusion. Being controlled by our feelings can be one of the most destructive enemies we face. You may be asking, "What does this have to do with building intimacy with our God?" My answer is that it could be everything.

Years ago, I personally faced one of these destructive giants. I lived with the enemy of fear. Fear can be a crippling feeling. It destroys your peace and robs you of joy. I had considered myself a thriving Christian. My husband was a deacon in the church. We were faithful to our quiet time. We both taught various Bible or enrichment studies. Over the years, we had led many ministries. But I had a "little" secret – I was afraid.

My thoughts and vain imaginations were unconstrained. I frequently mulled over the question, "What if?" What if we can't pay our house note? What if my husband should get sick, what if he died? What if my children were in an accident? As you can imagine, these "what ifs" were claiming a lot of my energy. I'd wake in the night imaging all kinds of disasters. I would often try to control my circumstances so that these perceived disasters would be minimized. I thought somehow that if I could control the pieces on my chessboard, I could control the outcome. What absolute nonsense.

Maybe you've never struggled with this enemy, but let me tell you, it can be gut wrenching, paralyzing, miserable. I wouldn't wish it on my worst enemy. Finally, it just became too much. I slumped to my knees and cried out to God, "Whatever it takes to get over this horrible captivity, I am willing." It was a turning point. I wanted freedom. I wanted to be released from this bondage.

I happened to be reading the book *Fresh Wind, Fresh Fire* when I came across this question: "What would your life look like revolutionized?"[12] I stopped and prayed, "God, how would you like to see my life revolutionized?" I grabbed a pen and began to write as I listened. There were several things; I can't even remember them all today, but I do remember this one. He said, "Get a mentor!" Within seconds, He had impressed on me the name of a woman I only knew casually. I thought, "She barely knows me." I resisted at first, but then reached for the phone. "Polly, this is Peggy Nicholson. I was wondering if

---

12   Jim Cymbala, *Fresh Wind, Fresh Fire*, (Grand Rapids, MI: Zondervan, 1997).

you'd consider mentoring me?" As if she'd been standing by the phone waiting for my call, she answered, "I'll see you Tuesday at 2:00." It was the beginning of my healing. Within two meetings, Polly had diagnosed my problem. I shared with her how I struggled with fear and worry. I thought perhaps she would have some compassion, perhaps she would suggest a counselor. I was stunned when she charged, "The problem is, you don't trust God." I felt like I had been slapped. I protested, "Of course, I trust God. I've been saved, baptized, and redeemed from the mud. I'm a servant of the living God! I trust Him!" She didn't flinch or back down. "Fear and trust cannot coexist. If you really trusted Him, you would relax and believe He always has your best interest at heart, no matter how it looks. You would not be dwelling on fearful thoughts. You would rest in His hammock. You would relax at His feet, knowing He loves you. He died for you. He can be trusted." Wow! That was the beginning of my surrender. I wrestled with God off and on for a few more months, but I was listening. I knew she was right. I had not given my complete trust to God. I could not say to Him with my hands open, "Whatever. Whatever the cost, whatever the loss." It took a little time to wrestle it through, but soon I found myself on my knees again with a new resolve. I opened my journal and wrote, "This is my irrevocable surrender. I will not take it back. I accept that Your will is perfect, and I bow to Your loving plan, whatever that is." It was actually hard to say, but at the same time, so freeing. I was done! No more waffling. I repeated and continue to repeat today, "I trust You, Lord! I choose to trust You now. My hands are open. Thy will be done."

This truly is our only path to peace in the midst of turmoil. We have not been promised a life free of pain and confusion, but, with faith and trust, we can rest through it. Coming to this point in your life should be your ultimate goal. I cannot claim that I no longer struggle when there is a crisis. Life can throw some pretty hard curves. When my much younger brother was hospitalized with COVID, I was fear-stricken. He was diabetic and was not vaccinated. I was out of the country when I got word from his wife that he was in critical condition. As I began my panicked prayers, I could hardly concentrate. I was, frankly, filled with terror. I was not resting in God's hammock at all. I was not trusting Him with the outcome. I wanted *my* will to be done. I adored my brother. He was my baby. I needed him to live! I fretted for a few miserable days. But finally, as I began to recognize my old enemy, I called on the Word of God.

When I am afraid, I put my trust in you. In God,
whose word I praise—in God I trust and am not afraid
(Psalm 56:3-4).

I began to repeat, "I trust you, Lord! I choose to trust You even now. I know Your will is perfect, and I surrender to it. My hands are open." I'd love to tell you that my brother lived, but, sadly, he did not. The truth is, my brother was going to die whether my hands were open or not. This is profound if you think about it. God ordains our days in advance. *Your eyes saw my unformed body. All the days ordained for me were written in your book before one of them came to be* (Psalm 139:16). We perceive we have some kind of control. We clench one fist behind our backs, hoping to protect some favorite thing or person. Somehow, we think, "I can't release these precious things to God. He may not go along with my plan. He may take me where I don't want to go. He may take what I don't want to give. His will may not be to my liking." May I encourage you, beloved believer, open your hands, both of them. He can be trusted. His plans are perfect even when we don't see it. This is faith. This is what we signed up for.

Without faith it is impossible to please God.
(Hebrews 11:6)

For we live by faith, not by sight. (2 Corinthians 5:7)

If and when you surrender your will to God, you will still have to deal with the effects of feelings. Feelings can be wonderful or paralyzing. You may not struggle with the feeling of fear as I did. Perhaps your enemy is anger or jealousy and envy. Whatever feeling holds you captive, there is only one way to control it. First, we must surrender our will to God; then we must look to God's Word to control our unruly feelings.

Like a city whose walls are broken through is a person who lacks self-control. (Proverbs 25:28)

Hannah Whitall Smith, in her book *The Christian's Secret to a Happy Life*, compares feelings to unruly children. If a mother in the nursery determines it is time for her children to go to bed, she must firmly hold to her resolve. Though the children whine and beg to stay up, the mother is unmoved. They are going to bed. It is unconditional. In the same way, we must deal with our feelings. Though they kick and scream for attention, they are ruled by us. Our will is king. We have decided! Our feelings belong to us, but they are not us. If they control us, we will sin![13]

So you may be saying, "Sounds great but impossible. My feelings are powerful and overwhelming." I agree! It is impossible to control all of our feelings. However, we can believe God when He tells us that all things are possible with Him.

> *The LORD makes firm the steps of the one who delights in him; though he may stumble, he will not fall for the LORD upholds him with his hand.*
> (Psalm 37:23-24)

Once when I was visiting with my mentor, I was explaining to her that I often worried about the future. I began a litany of "what ifs." What if the future held this or that? How could I bear it? She paused and simply said, "Don't go there." What? How is that possible? Well, it turns out, it is possible. Controlling our thoughts is our job. We are told to demolish arguments and pretensions that set themselves up against the knowledge of God. *Casting down imaginations, and every high thing that exalteth itself against the knowledge of God, and bringing into captivity every thought to the obedience of Christ* (2 Corinthians 10:5). I envision taking my useless, unruly feelings and throwing them down to the ground. Then it says we are to take every thought captive to the obedience of Christ Jesus. So, if I say no to fear, anger, jealousy, or other feelings, I can

---

13   Hannah Whitall Smith, *The Christian's Secret to a Happy Life*, (New York: Fleming H. Revell, 1888).

give those feelings to Christ where they are disposed of by our perfect Savior. Just don't go there! Who knew?

This spiritual condition is where we all want to be. We want to trust God with everything. We want to control our unmanageable feelings. We want peace. So how do the practices described in this book lead to this goal? The answer is that they are the only way.

Thy word is a lamp unto my feet and a light unto my path

CHAPTER 10

GUIDANCE FROM THE WORD OF GOD

All Scripture is God-breathed and is useful for teaching, rebuking, correcting and training in righteousness, so that the servant of God may be thoroughly equipped for every good work.
2 Timothy 3:16-17

How can we be equipped without equipment? The believer's equipment is the Holy Bible. It will lead us to life fulfillment. It will direct our steps. It will correct our wayward feelings and thoughts. It will protect us from making bad choices. *Your word is a lamp for my feet, a light on my path* (Psalm 119:105). *Do your best to present yourself to God as one approved, a worker who does not need to be ashamed and who correctly handles the word of truth* (2 Timothy 2:15).

As you move forward revising or developing your daily quiet time, don't forget your Bible. Reading and studying God's Word is as important as your daily prayer time. Knowing what God says, what He teaches, is essential to our spiritual health.

PREPARE

There are many choices for Bibles. You may already have one you love. If you are looking for a good study Bible, ask the Lord to lead you to the one He has chosen for you. I suggest you visit a Bible bookstore to see which fits you. Personally, I have chosen the Ryrie Study Bible in the NIV version. In the notes, I can quickly find who wrote the book, to whom it was written, the author's general purpose for writing, and where it was written. My husband prefers the American Standard Version. With a little research and maybe some recommendations from trusted fellow believers, you will find one that's right for you.

PRAY

Before you begin to read, pray. Ask the Lord to give you understanding and wisdom. In the front of my Bible, I have written the verse, *Open my eyes that I may see wonderful things in your law* (Psalm 119:18). If God does not open our eyes, we can comprehend nothing. Ask for the Holy Spirit's direction. Invite the Lord to speak to you through His Word and listen.

Psalm 46:10 says, *Be still, and know that I am God; I will be exalted among the nations, I will be exalted in the earth. Be still* or *cease striving* come from the Hebrew word "raphah," meaning to let drop, relax, let go, and be quiet.[14] Listening is critical. After all, we want to hear from heaven. We want God to open our eyes.

PLAN

I suggest that you have a reading/studying plan. Jumping around and reading randomly can be helpful, but studying from one book at a time is probably more effective. If you have the time, reading from one Old Testament book and one New Testament book can strengthen your understanding of both. For example, Genesis 1 and Matthew 1 on Monday and so on. It may also be helpful to read a psalm and a proverb each day if time permits. This was the habit of Billy Graham, so I conclude it must work.

Preparing to read God's Word by being still before Him will illuminate His message for you. Asking for His direction will give you a starting point. When you determine what book you will study, you may want to grab a journal and write down the main points in each chapter. We tend to retain what we write down better than only reading. As you read, if there is something you don't understand or simply want more clarity on, commentaries are readily available on your handy cell phone. Personally, I like Bible.org, provided by scholars from Dallas Theological Seminary. However, be intentional with your study and avoid distractions, especially those distractions that your phone presents. If this is problematic for you, as it is for me,

---

14   Debbie W. Wilson, "How to 'Be Still and Know I am God' (Even During Hard Times)," *Bible Study Tools*, May 20, 2022, https://www.biblestudytools.com/biblestudy/topical-studies/how-can-we-be-still-and-know-during-covid-19.html

consider purchasing a commentary book or two. This may help those of us ADHD people from wandering around in the wilderness checking on messages and to-do lists.

There are many Bible studies you can actually attend. Perhaps your church offers one. Homework may be involved, which is a great way to dig a little deeper and further your understanding of God's Word. I have enjoyed Bible Study Fellowship throughout the years, which is generally offered at a local church. It is extensive and will provide a great overview of several books of the Bible. It is also a wonderful place to take your young children to learn the Word of God. I might add it can also bring lovely, deep, godly friendships into your life. There are several organized Bible studies generally available, such as *Joy of Living*, *Community Bible Study*, and *Precepts for Life* by Kay Arthur, just to name a few. These are great adjuncts to your own personal study.

Reading Scripture out loud is also a useful tool to promote concentration and comprehension. When a passage speaks to you, stop and ask the Holy Spirit to magnify that truth and understanding. You may want to insert your name or a loved one's name inside the verse for personal application. For example, "We know that all things work together for good for my brother, Tim, who loves the Lord and is called according to His purpose."

Praying God's Word back to Him can be gratifying.[15] Here's an example using Ephesians 3:16: "Lord, I pray that you will

---

15   See Pray the Word Ministry, Mary Ann Bridgwater for further instruction.

grant my husband, according to the riches of your glory, to be strengthened with power through God's Spirit in the inner man." See Pray the Word Ministries, Mary Ann Bridgwater, for further instructions.

Paul wrote that God's Word is able to prepare us for every good work, so it is important that we read it, understand it, and even memorize it.

Bible Study

CHAPTER II

MEMORIZATION

*I have hidden your word in my heart that I might not
sin against you.*
Psalm 119:11

"The Hebrew word used for "hide" in this verse is *tsaphan*, which means to treasure, hoard, or cover. The word goes beyond our typical English definition of hide. It stretches past the idea of suppressing an object from view or storing an item in a cupboard or box. Only a possession of great value deserves to be cherished the way *tsaphan* suggests."[16] The Word of God is precious! We need to cherish it in our hearts. The Bible isn't a book that was designed to be casually read once and then put on a shelf. It's a living book that contains God's inspired words to guide our conduct and shape our beliefs. That means we need to know it and internalize it.

Your word is a lamp for my feet, a light on my path
(Psalm 119:105).

---

16 Annette Griffin, "Three Practical Ways to Transfer God's Word from Your Bible to Your Heart," *Christianity.com*, May 26, 2021, https://www.christianity.com/wiki/bible/practical-ways-to-transfer-gods-word-from-your-bible-to-your-heart.html

These commandments that I give you today are to be on your hearts. Impress them on your children. Talk about them when you sit at home and when you walk along the road, when you lie down and when you get up (Deuteronomy 6:6-7).

COMFORT

I am grateful that God has encouraged me through the years to memorize Scripture. It has comforted me and rescued me more times than I can count. Years ago, my husband, Art, was overcome by abdominal pain in the middle of the night. I rushed him to the emergency room. We waited in the lobby for several hours. During that time, my husband's appendix ruptured. They immediately rushed him in for emergency surgery. By this time, it was three or four in the morning. As I mentioned before, my weakness is fear-based sin. If I'm not careful, I will go straight to fear every time. I tense up. I imagine the worst. As I sat alone in the corridor, I began to panic. I quickly reached for my phone, planning to call dear friends to come and sit with me. But then I felt the Spirit say to me, "You can do this alone with just Me. You do not need anyone else." I put the phone down and began to relax. Passages I had memorized flooded my heart and mind, bathing my soul with calmness. I began to recite these verses and more.

When I am afraid, I put my trust in you. In God, whose word I praise—in God I trust and am not afraid. What can mere mortals do to me? (Psalm 56:3-4).

*God is our refuge and strength, an ever-present help
in trouble. Therefore we will not fear, though the
earth give way and the mountains fall into the heart
of the sea, though its waters roar and foam and the
mountains quake with their surging* (Psalm 46:1-3).

*I lift up my eyes to the mountains—where does my
help come from? My help comes from the Lord, the
Maker of heaven and earth. He will not let your foot
slip—he who watches over you will not slumber*
(Psalm 121:1-3).

I sat for the rest of the time, waiting in the corridor, reciting
Scripture to myself over and over again. I rested. I relaxed. I
praised. And I thanked God that He had encouraged me to
memorize those passages of Scripture. If for no other reason,
I needed them that night. Fortunately, my husband's surgery
was successful, and I had weathered the storm with God's
presence and His Holy Word. Unfortunately, most of us will,
at some point, encounter a similar crisis. When such a dark
night of the soul comes your way, be prepared. Hide God's
Word in your heart. Let His Word transform you and rescue
you. He is faithful.

COUNSEL

Another reason to memorize Scripture is to readily have the
truth on our lips. Since God's Word is the written authority
for all aspects of daily life, you are equipping yourself to be
a godly counselor by knowing verses that address specific

issues of life. For example, if asked what God's Word says about marriage, it would be good to have memorized verses on what God says about divorce, about what God says about leaving your mother and father and cleaving to each other, and what God says about submitting to one another.

WITNESS

Even more importantly, we need to have Scripture readily available to share our faith. If in a discussion with a friend who has questions about faith, we need to be prepared to defend it.

Do you know how to lead a searching heart to Christ's free gift of salvation? Can you use Scripture that is stored in your heart and mind to articulate your faith? The Bible admonishes us to do this: *Always be prepared to give an answer to everyone who asks you to give the reason for the hope that you have. But do this with gentleness and respect* (1 Peter 3:15).

The *Roman Road* has long provided a clear roadmap for the lay evangelist. It is a proven biblical tool to lead someone to saving faith.

For the wages of sin is death, but the gift of God is eternal life in Christ Jesus our Lord.
(Romans 6:23)

But God demonstrates his own love for us in this: While we were still sinners, Christ died for us.

(Romans 5:8)

If you declare with your mouth, 'Jesus is Lord,' and believe in your heart that God raised him from the dead, you will be saved. For it is with your heart that you believe and are justified, and it is with your mouth that you profess your faith and are saved.
(Romans 10:9-10)

For 'Everyone who calls on the name of the Lord will be saved.'
(Romans 10:13)

Therefore, since we have been justified through faith, we have peace with God through our Lord Jesus Christ.
(Romans 5:1)

Therefore, there is now no condemnation for those who are in Christ Jesus.
(Romans 8:1)

For I am convinced that neither death nor life, neither angels nor demons, neither the present nor the future, nor any powers, neither height nor depth, nor anything else in all creation, will be able to separate us from the love of God that is in Christ Jesus our Lord.
(Romans 8:38-39)

Therefore, since we have justified through faith, we have peace with God through our Lord Jesus Christ. (Romans 5:1)

Being familiar with your Bible can enrich your life and the lives of others.

FIGHT TEMPTATION

Scripture retained will help to fight temptation. When we are tempted to sin, it is important to know what the Word of God says about that sin. For example, if you are tempted to lie, you would want to know what God says about liars.

The LORD detests lying lips, but he delights in people who are trustworthy. (Proverbs 12:22)

Do not lie to each other, since you have taken off your old self with its practices. (Colossians 3:9)

If you are tempted to cheat on your income tax or your employer's expense report, you would want to know what God says about stealing. God's Word has an answer for every sin you are facing.

God's Word protects us from destruction. Sin will eventually destroy us, so the Bible says we must master it. Scripture hidden in our hearts will protect us from Satan's traps.

Be alert and of sober mind. Your enemy the devil prowls around like a roaring lion looking for someone to devour. (1 Peter 5:8)

If you do what is right, will you not be accepted? But if you do not do what is right, sin is crouching at your door; it desires to have you, but you must rule over it. (Genesis 4:7)

COMFORT FOR OTHERS

The Word hidden in our hearts can be a comfort and counsel for loved ones. John Piper wrote, "The times when people need you to give them comfort and counsel do not always coincide with the times you have your Bible handy. Not only that, the very word of God spoken spontaneously from your heart has unusual power. Proverbs 25:11 says, A word fitly spoken is like apples of gold in a setting of silver. That is a beautiful way of saying, 'When the heart full of God's love can draw on the mind full of God's word, timely blessings flow from the mouth.'"[17]

Scripture is the most comforting thing you can give when someone has lost a loved one or has received devastating news. The Word of God is powerful and reaches down into our very souls. If you are prepared to meet a hurting friend with life-giving Scripture, you will speak hope into their weary hearts. Our words are usually flimsy at best when someone is brokenhearted, but God's Word is nourishment to the soul.

---

17   John Piper, "Why Memorize Scripture?" desiringGod, September 5, 2006, https://desiringgod.org/articles/why-memorize-scripture.

CHAPTER 12

REWARDS

However, as it is written: 'What no eye has seen,
what no ear has heard, and what no human mind has
conceived' — the things God has prepared for those
who love him.
1 Corinthians 2:9

"The first step toward applying God's Word in our lives is reading it. Our goal in reading is to get to know God, to learn His ways, and to understand His purpose for this world and for us individually. In reading the Bible, we learn about God's interactions with humanity throughout history, His plan of redemption, His promises, and His character. We see what the Christian life looks like. The knowledge of God we glean from Scripture serves as an invaluable foundation for applying the Bible's principles for life."[18]

God has graciously provided the Holy Spirit, our Counselor, and the Holy Word of God, our divine directive. Together, these

---

18   Unknown author, "What is the key to applying the Bible to my life?" GotQuestions, accessed July 3, 2023, https://gotquestions.org/applying-the-Bible.html

powerful gifts of God will transform your life. These are not just hollow promises. This is a holy promise. Scripture *will* transform the willing believer. *Taste and see that the LORD is good* (Psalm 34:8). The Word is not just for us to read or study; it's the living Word. It changes us, motivates us, and inspires us to allow God to chip off our rough edges, leaving us with His creative renovation. Who doesn't want to be renovated by our loving Creator? God, please don't leave us like we are! Change us! Please make us new as you've promised in your Word. Applying God's Word to your life will challenge you daily to excellence.

Praying and Bible study are the primary ways we develop intimacy with our God. Setting aside intentional time is key to this fulfilling, satisfying relationship. Entering into His presence is a holy time. It is precious and should be guarded diligently.

We must all get to know God personally. We must speak with Him daily. We must study His Word. These practices will lead us to know Him. We cannot trust someone we don't know. It takes intentional time to build that kind of intimacy. If you haven't begun yet, let me encourage you to do so. The benefits are incalculable.

Applying both the prayer discipline and Bible study disciplines to your daily routine will set you on the course to intimacy with our Maker. Knowing God and being fully known will teach us to trust the hand of our living God. If this is your goal, then make a commitment to start today. Don't give up when you're feeling dry. Push through and stand firm. The rewards are boundless. Press on, faithful pilgrim.

QUESTIONS FOR REFLECTION

- What changes are you willing to make to develop the discipline of daily sacred quiet time?

- Do you remember to honor God as holy?

- Do you enter His presence with reverence?

- Whom do you need to forgive?

- Have you forgotten to pray for yourself?

- What burdens you? What keeps you up at night? Have you laid it at His feet? Have you left it there?

- Have you neglected to pray specifically for your husband and family members?

- Is there someone God has brought to mind with whom you need to share Christ's salvation story?

- In which area (praise, thanksgiving, confession, supplication, or intercession) is your prayer time weak and in need of reviving?

- Have you offered God your will?

- Have you surrendered it all?

- Is your Bible reading erratic and confusing?

- Do you have a plan?

- Have you considered joining an organized Bible Study?

- Have you made a plan to hide God's Word in your heart?

ABOUT THE AUTHOR

Peggy Nicholson is a wife and mother of two and currently a grandmother to six grandchildren. She is married to Art Nicholson, a native Houstonian and a member of Houston's First Baptist Church since 1979. She is a native of Louisville, Kentucky, and has resided in Houston, Texas, for the last 42 years. Peggy has led a marriage class at Houston's First Baptist Church for the past nine years. She loves discipling women of all ages and is passionate about teaching them the life-transforming principles found in this book.

Contact Peggy at: pegrnich@gmail.com